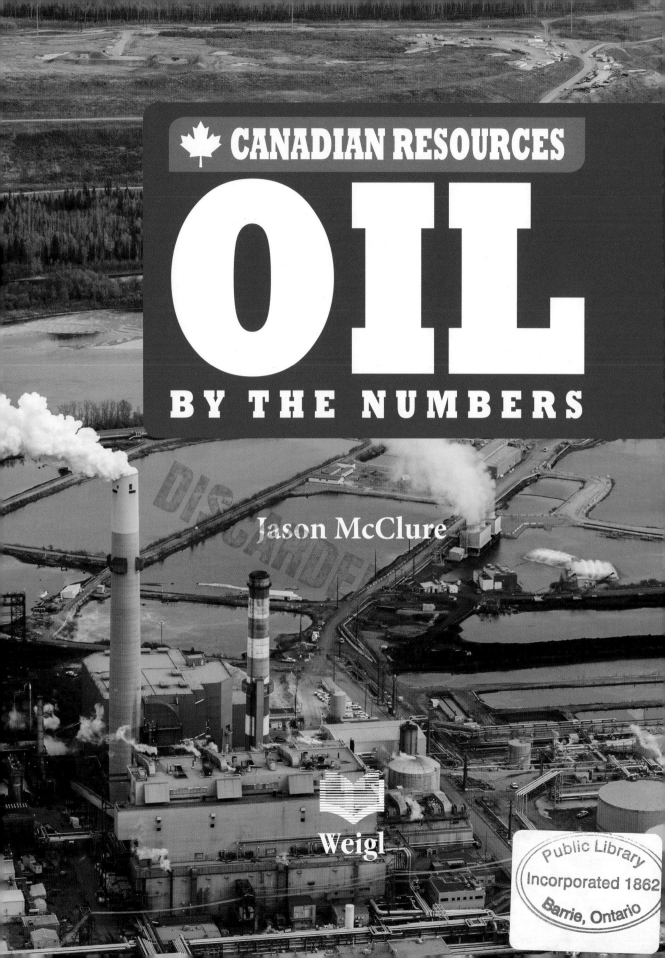

CANADIAN RESOURCES

OIL

BY THE NUMBERS

Jason McClure

Weigl

Published by Weigl Educational Publishers Limited
6325 10th Street SE
Calgary, Alberta, Canada
T2H 2Z9

Website: www.weigl.ca

Library and Archives Canada Cataloguing in Publication available
upon request. Fax 403-233-7769 for the attention of the Publishing
Records department.

ISBN 978-1-77071-268-3 (hardcover)

ISBN 978-1-77071-269-0 (softcover)

ISBN 978-1-77071-270-6 (multi-user eBook)

Printed in the United States of America
in North Mankato, Minnesota

1 2 3 4 5 6 7 8 9 0 17 16 15 14 13

072013
WEP130613

Weigl acknowledges Getty Images and Alamy as the primary image
suppliers for this title. Every reasonable effort has been made to
trace ownership and to obtain permission to reprint copyright
material. The publishers would be pleased to have any errors or
omissions brought to their attention so that they may be corrected
in subsequent printings.

We acknowledge the financial support of the Government of Canada
through the Canada Book Fund for our publishing activities.

Project Coordinator
Heather Kissock

Art Director
Terry Paulhus

CANADIAN RESOURCES

OIL

BY THE NUMBERS

CONTENTS

Oil companies set up large platforms called derricks to begin drilling.

Oil Resources

"Although most Americans don't know it, the U.S. gets more oil from Canada than it does from the entire Middle East." Jeff Goodell, U.S. author

Oil is one of Canada's best-known **natural resources**. Located in underground rock and sand, this resource is in demand all over the world. Oil is a fuel. It is used to power everything from cars and airplanes to houses and cities. Countries that do not have oil as a resource rely on oil-rich countries, such as Canada, to supply them with their oil. As needed as this resource is, accessing it creates many problems for the environment. Oil companies are always searching for new ways to make the process more friendly to the environment.

How Oil is Formed

Oil is a **fossil fuel**. It takes millions of years for it to form.

Plants and animals die and sink to the sea floor.

Layers of dirt and sediment cover the remains.

Heat and pressure turn the remains into fossil fuels, including oil.

Earth's Oil

Where oil is found depends on the **geology** of an area. **Crude oil** is found in places where animal and plant life existed hundreds of millions of years ago. Most of the organisms that formed the world's oil were marine animals and plants. Areas such as Saudi Arabia and northern Alberta used to be covered with water and were very rich in marine animal and plant life. While these areas are no longer covered in water, the remains of the animals and plants that once lived there have become part of the underlying earth. As a result, these areas contain much of the world's oil.

Oil is not found in large underground pools. Instead, after it is formed, it seeps into surrounding rock and sand.

World Oil Reserves

Oil is found in large amounts in many places around the world. However, oil is a **non-renewable resource**. Once it is used, it cannot be replaced. This chart indicates how many barrels of oil the world's oil-rich countries are estimated to have remaining in their known **reserves**.

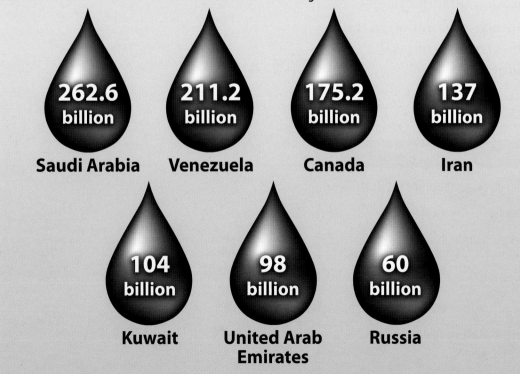

262.6 billion — **Saudi Arabia**

211.2 billion — **Venezuela**

175.2 billion — **Canada**

137 billion — **Iran**

104 billion — **Kuwait**

98 billion — **United Arab Emirates**

60 billion — **Russia**

Oil in Canada

Oil has been found in all of Canada's provinces and territories. However, most of Canada's oil supply comes from Alberta's oil sands. In fact, Alberta has about 98 percent of Canada's oil supply. In recent years, reserves in Saskatchewan have also begun to produce large amounts of oil.

The waters around Canada have also been proven to be rich in oil. Oil companies have set up several offshore drilling sites off the coast of Newfoundland. There is also much exploration in the Arctic Ocean, around the Beaufort Sea.

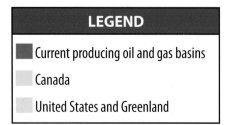

LEGEND

- Current producing oil and gas basins
- Canada
- United States and Greenland

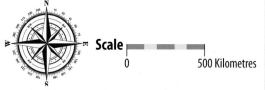

Scale
0   500 Kilometres

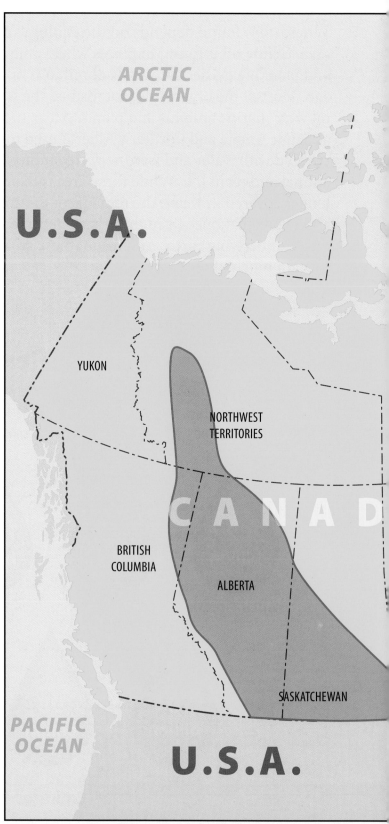

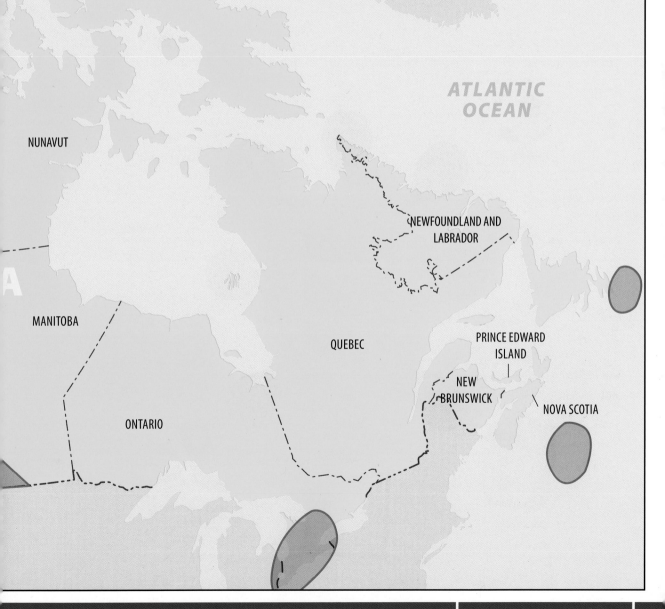

GREENLAND

ATLANTIC
OCEAN

NUNAVUT

NEWFOUNDLAND AND
LABRADOR

A

MANITOBA

QUEBEC

PRINCE EDWARD
ISLAND

NEW
BRUNSWICK

NOVA SCOTIA

ONTARIO

Oil Products

The crude oil that is found in Canada has many uses. Oil provides heat for homes and power to run factories. It also provides the raw materials to make **petrochemicals** and plastics. The greatest use of oil by individual people, however, is the automobile. In North America, two thirds of all oil is used for transportation.

Products made with Oil

Oil is used to make a wide variety of products. When used in petrochemicals, oil can help manufacture items ranging from plastic bottles to laundry detergents.

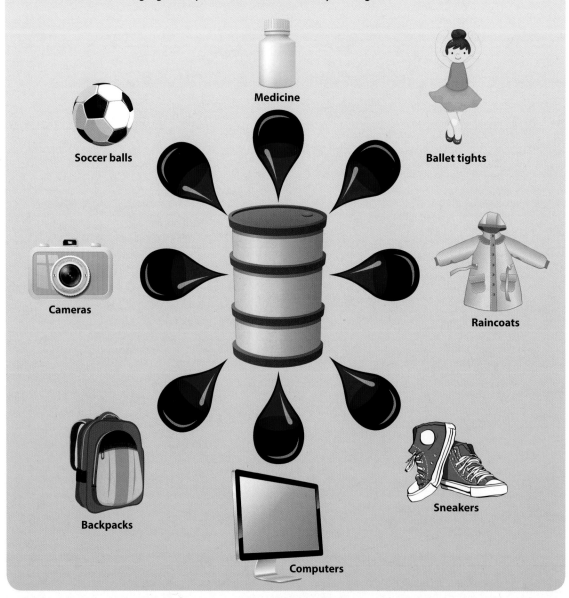

Medicine

Ballet tights

Soccer balls

Cameras

Raincoats

Backpacks

Computers

Sneakers

Oil as Fuel

In 2011, there were more than one billion cars on roads worldwide. Most of these vehicles require gasoline to operate. Gasoline is made from oil. To make gasoline, companies take oil and refine it. This means they separate the ingredients that make up the oil. One of these ingredients is gasoline. Crude oil is the source of other fuels as well.

Where Does a Barrel of Oil Go?

Oil is often stored in large metal containers called barrels. A barrel holds 159 litres of oil. These 159 litres can make approximately 170 litres of oil-based products.

73.3 litres
Gasoline, for use by small road vehicles

38.0 litres
Diesel fuel, for use by large vehicles

30.4 litres
Other products, such as petrochemicals

14.9 litres
Jet fuel, for use by aircraft

6.5 litres
Liquid petroleum gas, for use in heating homes

6.4 litres
Heavy fuel oil, for use in manufacturing

Making Gasoline

Making gasoline is a long process. First, the crude oil has to be removed from the ground. It then has to be transferred to a refinery. Here, it must be processed so that the gasoline is separated from the crude oil and made ready for use.

2

Drilling
Once oil is found, drilling machines are set up. They drill into the ground toward the oil source. When the drilling reaches the oil, the oil is pumped to the surface.

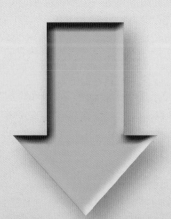

1

Finding the Oil
Scientists drill for cores, or samples, of rock deep underground. The scientists study these cores to see if the conditions might be present for oil to have formed.

Shipping the Crude

The oil then has to be shipped to the refinery for processing. If the oil is mixed with sand, it is shipped by truck. If it is in a liquid state, it travels through a pipeline to the refinery.

Processing the Crude

When the crude oil arrives at the refinery, it is put through a system of furnaces. The heat in the furnaces separates the oil into its different parts and turns it into the different fuels, including gasoline. The gasoline then goes through a treatment process to get it ready for use.

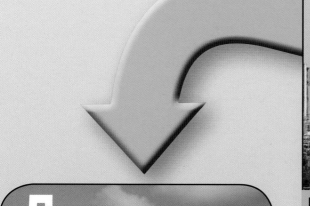

Storage

The gasoline is placed in large storage tanks. When it has been sold, it is shipped to customers by pipeline.

Oil as Power

Oil provides power for more than cars. Industry uses oil as an energy source as well. The type of oil that industry uses for energy is called heavy oil. Heavy oil is not refined like gasoline. It is thick and contains more **pollutants**. Oil companies actually use heavy oil to make gasoline. It is burned to create the heat needed in the oil refining process. Other industries that rely on heavy oil to create heat include the pulp and paper industry and the electricity industry.

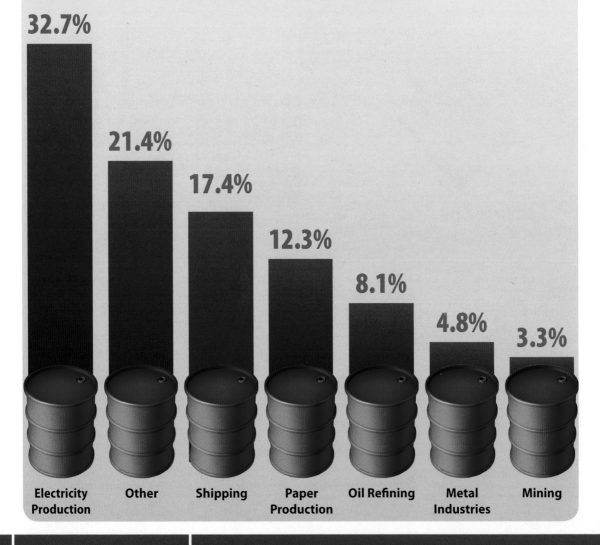

Heavy Oil Use by Industry

In Canada, electricity production makes up the greatest percentage of industry's heavy oil use each year. However, several other industries also burn heavy oil to power their operations. This chart shows which industries use Canada's heavy oil and how much they use.

32.7% — Electricity Production
21.4% — Other
17.4% — Shipping
12.3% — Paper Production
8.1% — Oil Refining
4.8% — Metal Industries
3.3% — Mining

Heating Homes

Canada is a northern country. It relies on energy to make living in a northern climate possible. In winter, many people use oil to heat their homes. Oil is known to provide the hottest flame of any fossil fuel. This means that it heats up an area faster than other forms of energy. Heating oil is used mostly in Ontario, Quebec, and the Atlantic Provinces, in areas that have limited access to other types of heating. In one year, approximately 3.5 billion litres of oil will be used to heat Canadian homes.

Canada's cold winter temperatures require Canadians to rely on heating systems. Oil is just one resource used to keep buildings warm through the season.

Oil Consumption by Country

Even though Canada has a relatively small population, its people and industries use more oil than many other countries. In fact, Canada is one of the top 10 consumers of oil in the world. In 2011, Canada used approximately 2.3 million barrels of oil per day to heat homes, power factories, and operate vehicles.

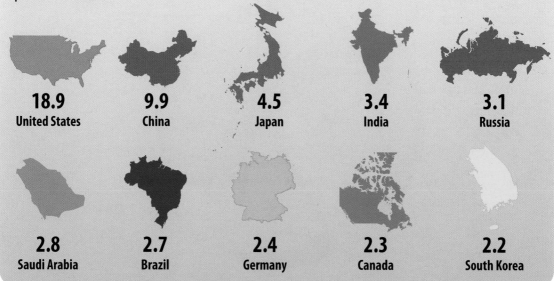

18.9	**9.9**	**4.5**	**3.4**	**3.1**
United States	China	Japan	India	Russia
2.8	**2.7**	**2.4**	**2.3**	**2.2**
Saudi Arabia	Brazil	Germany	Canada	South Korea

The Oil Industry

Oil production is part of Canada's energy industry. This industry also includes natural gas and electricity production. The energy industry contributes much to the Canadian economy. In 2010 alone, it made more than $84 billion. This was about seven percent of the country's total income. A large portion of this money came from **export** sales.

Large drilling platforms are installed offshore to drill for oil found on the ocean floor.

Energy in the Canadian Economy

Canada's industries are divided into sectors that describe the products being sold. The energy industry is part of the natural resources sector. This sector also includes the forestry and mining industries. Goods coming out of the natural resources sector make up about 11.5 percent of Canada's total yearly income. The energy industry, however, provides the largest percentage of sales within the sector.

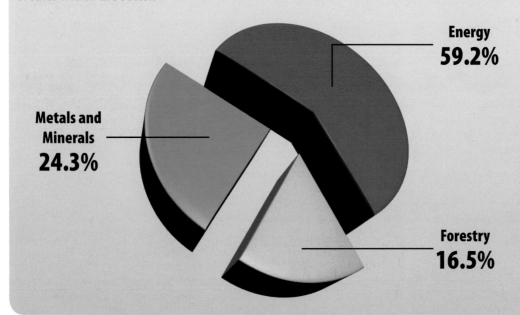

Energy 59.2%

Metals and Minerals 24.3%

Forestry 16.5%

Oil Exports

Oil exports are big business in Canada, accounting for $87.1 billion alone in 2011. Approximately 99 percent of this oil is sold to the United States. Canada ships much of its oil through pipelines that connect to oil refineries along the Gulf of Mexico and the U.S. Midwest.

The Pipeline Network

Canada has an advantage over other countries when supplying oil. Sharing a border with the United States makes it much simpler to transport the product. Pipelines are considered the safest and most efficient way to move oil from one place to another. Today, there are about 3.4 million kilometres of pipeline operating in Canada and the United States.

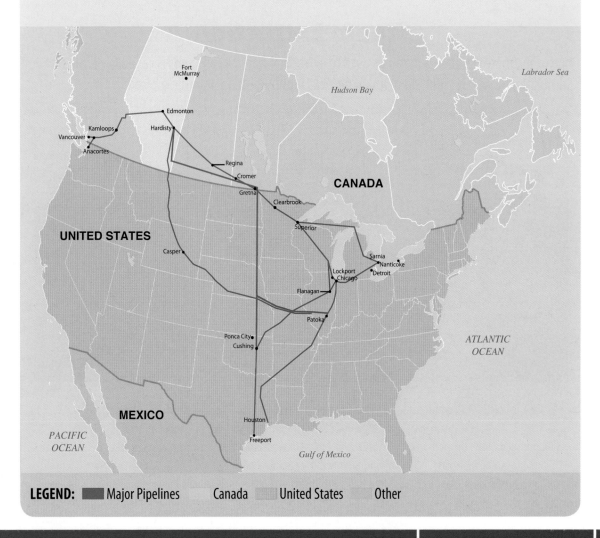

LEGEND: Major Pipelines　Canada　United States　Other

Technology in the Oil Sands

Alberta's oil sands are currently one of the most active oil operations in the world.

The oil industry depends on technology in many ways. As the resource is buried deep within the ground, technology is needed to find and remove the oil from the ground. Oil companies have to find ways to remove the oil while limiting their environmental impact.

Steam Extraction

One of the more traditional methods used to extract oil from the oil sands is called Cyclic Steam Stimulation (CSS). This method relies on oil jacks pumping steam into the ground.

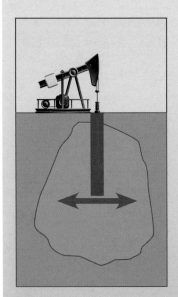

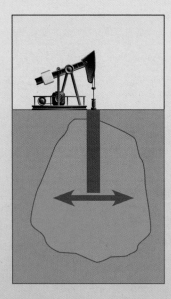

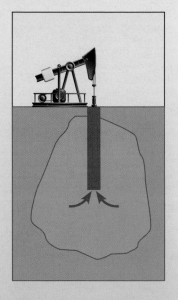

1 First, a hole is drilled into the oil sands. Hot steam is then pumped down the hole. This steam can be pumped continuously for days.

2 The steam heats up the oil causing it to melt from its tar-like state into a more liquid form. The steamed oil is left to sit for a few days.

3 The newly-created liquid oil is pumped out and refined.

Alberta's oil sands are Canada's largest source of oil. This oil, however, is not found in liquid form. Special processes have to be used to separate the oil from the oil sands. Many of these processes use water, in the form of steam, to lift the oil from the oil sands.

In recent years, oil sands companies have begun using a technique called Steam Assisted Gravity Drainage (SAGD) to separate oil from the oil sands. In SAGD, two holes are drilled into the ground. Instead of being drilled straight down, however, these holes are drilled horizontally. One hole is drilled a few metres above the other one. Steam is pumped into the top hole. This melts the oil, which then drips down into the second hole where it is pumped out and refined.

SAGD uses much more water than CSS, but it also allows more oil to be taken. Once used, the water is polluted and must be cleaned and recycled. Some oil companies in Alberta claim they are able to recycle more than 90 percent of the water they use.

Experts believe new projects and better technology will help the oil sands move from producing about 1.3 million barrels of oil each day to about 3 million barrels by 2018.

Working with Oil

In 2010, Canada's energy sector employed about 500,000 workers directly and indirectly. At least 264,000 of these people worked directly in the field. In the oil industry, direct workers include those who drill for oil and work in processing plants and refineries. Indirect employees hold jobs at gas stations and oil plant construction sites. The oil industry in Canada is one of the highest paying industries. Each year, oil companies pay billions of dollars in salaries.

Oil Industry Jobs

The oil industry needs a variety of workers to operate. Some work directly in the oil fields. Others provide the support needed to keep the work flowing.

Engineering

Several types of engineers, including process engineers and production engineers, work in the oil industry. These people locate oil sources and plan the best ways to access the oil.

Support Services

Support workers handle the materials that process workers extract. These workers include truck drivers, inspectors, and general labourers.

Process Workers

Process workers are the people directly involved in getting the oil from the ground. Rig workers and production operators belong to this work group.

Executives and Management

Managers and executives make decisions on behalf of the company and its employees. The company president, along with vice-presidents and supervisors, make up this part of an oil company.

Oil Industry Jobs

There is a wide range of jobs within the oil industry. Each job has different tasks to perform and requires a certain type of training.

Surface Land Agent

Duties: Buys land for oil companies, works with the community to address concerns
Education: 2 years of college training

Surface land agents work with oil companies and communities. Their job is to talk to the people who may be affected by an oil company's work in an area. They also take the concerns of the people to the oil company.

Pipeline Worker

Duties: Monitors pipelines for leaks, repairs problems, and conducts simple tests
Education: High school diploma, on-the-job training

Pipeline workers build giant pipes that carry oil from one place to another. With more than 100,000 kilometres of pipelines in Canada, pipeline workers are always busy making sure that Canada's pipelines are safe and working properly.

Truck Driver

Duties: Operates large trucks to help remove materials from the work site
Education: Special driver's license

Digging up oil often involves moving a great deal of earth and rock. Oil fields use large dump trucks to carry this material away. To drive such giant trucks, drivers must be very skilled. They train a long time to learn how to operate such big machines safely.

Managing Oil

Oil is a resource people use for many things, but accessing the oil can cause damage to the environment. Forests may need to be removed to build an oil drilling plant. Mountains may need to be blasted. These environments and the organisms that live there can be seriously affected by the process of extracting, processing, and shipping oil.

Governments

Governments set rules that guide how and where oil companies can work. These rules tell the companies how big their work site can be and how they must clean any pollution they create. These rules also indicate where drilling is not allowed, such as in protected natural areas.

Individuals

Due to the harm oil development causes the environment, many people are beginning to watch their use of oil and oil products. They try to carpool or walk when travelling short distances. Some people are taking action to ensure that Canada's oil resources are being used in a responsible way. They work with environmental groups and governments to make sure oil companies are being as environmentally friendly as possible.

The exploration and production processes needed to make oil usable also have an impact on the air. Oil refineries produce **greenhouse gases**, which have been directly linked to climate change. Many different groups, as well as the government, work with oil companies to make sure that Canada's oil resources are used properly and that the environment is affected as little as possible.

Companies

Oil companies are aware that their work harms the environment. Many have started programs to restore the land they dig and reduce the amount of greenhouse gases they produce. They hire environmental experts to help them find better ways to access oil and invest much money and time into researching new extraction methods.

Environmental Groups

Environmental groups work with governments and oil companies to make sure that the companies are following the rules. These groups also look for ecosystems that need to be protected and bring that information to the government and the oil companies. The work of environmental groups helps protect the environment while still allowing oil companies to do their work.

Quiz

How much oil does Canada have in its reserves?

175.2 billion barrels

Where are the majority of Canada's oil resources found?

Alberta

How do most people use oil in their daily lives?

Driving their cars

How much oil does a barrel hold?

159 litres

What is most of Canada's heavy oil used for?

Generating electricity

Which country is the largest consumer of oil?

United States

How does Canada ship most of its oil to the United States?

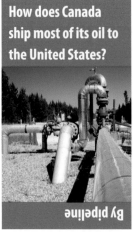

By pipeline

How is water used in the oil sands extraction process?

To produce steam

Further Resources

Websites to check out!

Alberta Culture
http://history.alberta.ca/oilsands/resources/
docs/fact-sheets-for-kids-2012.pdf

Kids Zone
www.kidzone.ercb.ca/noflash.html

How Stuff Works
http://science.howstuffworks.com/
environmental/green-science/oil-sands.htm

Activity

Make a Lava Lamp

Materials Needed: Vegetable oil, water, clear 2-litre plastic bottle, food colouring, glitter, Alka Seltzer tablets, flashlight

Oil and water do not mix. This is because oil is less dense, or lighter, than water. Oil floats on top of water. In this activity, use this fact to create your own lava lamp. Use a cooking oil such as vegetable oil.

1. Fill the bottle about one quarter full of water. Fill the rest of the bottle with the vegetable oil. Let the oil separate from the water and settle.
2. Add a few drops of food colouring. Watch the food colouring settle at the bottom of the bottle. Once the food colouring has settled, break two Alka Seltzer tablets in half and drop them into the bottle.
3. Shine the flashlight through the back to see the lava lamp colours even better. As the Alka Seltzer dissolves, the effect will stop. Add more Alka Seltzer to see it again.

Key Words

crude oil: a dark, thick oil that has not been refined

export: a product shipped to another country

fossil fuel: an energy source formed from the remains of plants and animals that lived long ago

geology: the study of rocks and rock formations

greenhouse gases: any gases that contribute to global warming

natural resources: naturally made materials that can be used by people

non-renewable resource: a resource that is not replaced in nature after it is used

petrochemicals: a range of products made from chemicals that are produced during the processing of crude oil

pollutants: waste materials that contaminate the air, land, and water

reserves: resources known or believed to exist in a certain location

Index